Introduction

Japanese cuisine has become increasingly popular the world over. The natural ingredients and simple cooking styles exemplified in Japanese cuisine appeal to a more ecologically-conscious audience. Contrary to popular belief, Japanese cooking is quite easy. All you need to bear in mind is not to overcook. The philosophy behind Japanese cooking is that eating raw or near raw food is the best way to appreciate its real taste. In this selection of recipes I try to show the way Japanese food is prepared at home rather than in a restaurant so that you can easily follow and enjoy what may at first seem a complex cuisine. Wherever possible I have also tried to restrict ingredients to those readily available.

I would like to correct a few English words widely used in Japanese and oriental cuisine generally. *Hashi*, for example, are elegant pieces of cutlery which are *not* called chopsticks since they are never used to chop food. And the word *soy*, as in *soy* sauce, is from the regional dialect of the southern island of Kyushu, whence the sauce made its way west. The proper Japanese name for the sauce, however, is *shoyu*. In the text I prefer to use the correct terms *hashi* and *shoyu*.

A note on measures

Spoon measurements are level except where otherwise indicated. Seasonings can of course be adjusted according to taste. Recipes are for four.

P9-ECM-939

Gohan

Boiled Rice

A traditional Japanese person starts a hard working day with rice and soup. Japanese rice is a short grain, sticky variety which is almost always plain boiled. In Japanese boiled rice is called *gohan* which also means "a meal." One cup of rice will make 2 – 3 bowls of boiled rice, sufficient for 2 people. Wash the rice very thoroughly, changing the water a few times until it appears clear. Place the washed rice in a deep saucepan with 20 percent more cold water than rice (if I cup of rice is used the water should come about $1/2$ inch above the rice), cover and leave for 10 minutes before cooking. Place the pan on a high heat and bring to a boil. Lower the heat and simmer gently for about 15 minutes until all the water has been absorbed. Remove from heat and leave the saucepan with the lid on for about 10 minutes before serving.

Miso Shiru

Bean Paste Soup

What really distinguishes Japanese cuisine from any other is the use of soup. The soup stock, called *dashi*, is fish flavored, made from *konbu* (dried kelp), *katsuobushi* (dried bonito flakes), or *niboshi* (dried tiny sardines). *Konbu* makes the most delicate

flavor of all and is normally used with *katsuobushi*, while *niboshi* is the strongest flavored and good for making strong-tasting soups such as this one.

---

2 cups water
1 oz niboshi *or* konbu *and a handful of* katsuobushi
1 packet ($^1/_3$ oz) cut and dried wakame *(seaweed)*
2 tbsp miso *(soya bean paste)*
1 cake firm tofu *(bean curd)*
2 spring onions, finely chopped

Put the *niboshi* and the water in a saucepan. Bring quickly to a boil and simmer for 5–10 minutes. Remove from heat, strain through a fine sieve and discard the *niboshi*. If *konbu* and *katsuobushi* are used instead, soak the *konbu* for 10 minutes, bring to a boil, then add the *katsuobushi*, boil for a few seconds only, remove from the heat and leave to stand for 1 minute, or until the *katsuobushi* settles down to the bottom of the pan. Strain the *dashi* through a clean gauze cloth.

Soak the *wakame* in plenty of cold water for 5–10 minutes until fully expanded. Put the *miso* in a small bowl and dilute with a few spoonfuls of the stock. Return the pan of stock to the low heat and add the diluted *miso*. Cut the *tofu* into small cubes and add to the pan with the *wakame*. Just before boiling point remove the soup from the heat and add the finely chopped spring onions. Serve hot, in warmed individual soup bowls with hot plain boiled rice.

Sumashi-Jiru

Clear Soup

This is a Japanese consommé. You can use any white fish, *tofu*, chicken breast or even very fine noodles instead of prawns.

---

4 headless uncooked prawns, defrosted if frozen
or 1 chicken breast
1 tsp salt
a little cornstarch, for coating
3 cups dashi (see page 4)
1 tsp shoyu
2 spring onions, finely chopped

Wash and shell the prawns but retain the shell on the end of the tail. Remove the black vein on the back. Pat dry. Season the prawns with a little of the salt, then dust with cornstarch. Plunge them into a saucepan of boiling water for 1 minute, then drain and set aside. Heat the *dashi* in a medium-size saucepan and season with the *shoyu* and remaining salt. Divide the prawns equally between 4 warmed soup bowls and pour the *dashi* over. Garnish with the chopped spring onions and serve hot.

If you use chicken, slice diagonally into bite-size pieces and cook the same way as prawns, but for 2-3 minutes.

Chawan-Mushi

Thick Egg Soup

This makes an excellent, filling starter. It is also a nourishing dish for infants and old people and a soothing meal when you feel unwell. Traditional *chawan mushi* cups are available at Japanese and other oriental food stores but you can substitute with coffee mugs or tea cups.

4 oz boneless chicken	4 snow peas
breast, skinned	2 cups dashi (see page 4)
saké (rice wine)	1 tsp sugar
shoyu	3 eggs, beaten
4 prawns	4 small button mushrooms,
salt	wiped

Thinly slice the chicken, then sprinkle with a little *saké* and *shoyu*. Wash and shell the prawns, leaving the tail shell on. Take out the black vein. Sprinkle the prawns with a little *saké* and a pinch of salt. Plunge the snow peas into a saucepan of lightly salted water for 1 minute, then drain. Heat the *dashi* in a medium-size saucepan, add 1/2 tsp salt, 1 tsp sugar and 1 tbsp *shoyu*. Remove from the heat and leave to cool for 15 minutes, then slowly add the beaten eggs. Divide the chicken, prawns, mushrooms and snow peas equally between 4 *chawan mushi* cups or coffee mugs and pour in the egg soup.

Put the covered cups (use tinfoil to cover the coffee mugs) in a steamer and steam vigorously for 2 minutes. Lower the heat and steam for a further 12–15 minutes, or until the juice runs clear when the thickened soup is pierced with a *hashi* or fork. Alternatively, put the cups or mugs in a shallow baking dish half-filled with hot water and cook in the oven at 425°F for 5 minutes, then at 350°F for 20–25 minutes, or until set. Serve the soup immediately.

Sunomono

Vinegared Salad

This classic Japanese vinegared salad of finely sliced cucumber and soft *wakame* (seaweed) can be served as an hors d'oeuvre or as a refreshing accompaniment to a main meal.

1 cucumber	2 pkts (½ oz) cut wakame
1 tsp salt	(dried young seaweed)
	1 – 1½ inch piece fresh
	root ginger
Sanbaizu sauce	
3 tbsp rice vinegar	1 tbsp shoyu
1 tbsp sugar	1 pinch salt

Halve the cucumber lengthways and slice very thinly to make half-moons. Sprinkle with salt and leave for 10 minutes. Using your hands, squeeze out the water from the cucumber slices, and set aside. Soak the *wakame* in cold water for 5–10 minutes until fully expanded. Drain, lightly blanch in boiling water, then rinse under cold running water. Drain well and squeeze out any excess water with your hands. If the *wakame* is not already chopped, cut away the hard spine-like strip, and chop the soft part into 1 inch lengths. Peel and finely shred the ginger, then

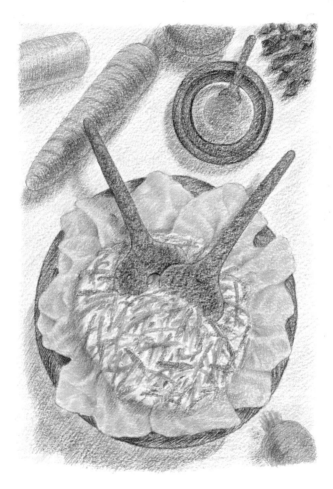

place in a bowl of ice-cold water to crisp. Put all the ingredients for the sauce in a bowl, mix well together, then add the sliced cucumber and *wakame*. Toss well. Transfer the salad to individual salad bowls, shaping it into neat mounds. Sprinkle the shredded ginger over the top of the salad.

Wafu Salada

Japanese Salad

1/2 medium carrot, peeled	*1 celery stalk*
1/2 cucumber	*lettuce leaves, to serve*
1/2 red onion	
Gomadaré dressing	
2 *tbsp* tahini (sesame paste)	*1 tbsp* dashi (see page 4)
or peanut butter	or water
2 *tbsp* rice vinegar	*1 tbsp* shoyu
pinch of chilli oil (optional)	salt

Shred the carrot, cucumber, red onion and celery into about 2 inch long pieces, and place them in a large bowl of ice-cold water to crisp up while preparing the remaining ingredients. Mix all the ingredients for the dressing together in a bowl with a pinch of salt to taste and set aside. Drain the shredded vegetables and place back into the large bowl. Pour the *gomadaré* sauce over the salad and toss well so that the color of the vegetables is spread evenly. Arrange the salad on a bed of lettuce in a large salad bowl.

Karashi-Ae

Salad with Mustard Dressing

Many Japanese salads are very quick and easy to prepare. This recipe is one of the simplest.

I tbsp saké
$^1/_2$ lb or I can baby clams, cleaned
3 tbsp shoyu, plus I tsp
I tsp mustard
$^1/_2$ lb spinach, washed and trimmed
I tsp sesame seeds
salt

Rinse the cockles under cold running water and place in a small saucepan. Add the *saké* and heat through. Drain the cockles, reserving the juice. Put 3 tbsp *shoyu* and the mustard in a bowl and mix together. Add the cockles. Cook the spinach in lightly salted boiling water for 30 seconds, then drain and plunge immediately into a bowl of ice-cold water. Drain again and squeeze out any excess water. Cut roughly into bite-size pieces and pour over I tsp *shoyu*. Put the cockles, spinach and the cockle juice in a bowl and mix well. Arrange a quarter of the mixture in small individual bowls to form a small mound, and serve.

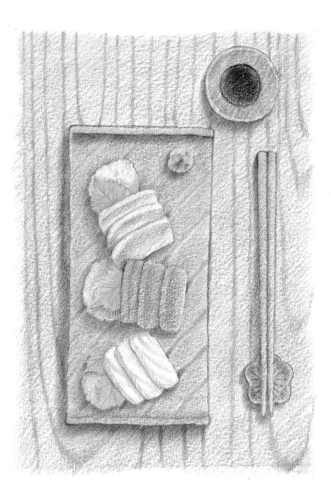

Sashimi

Assorted Raw Fish

Sashimi is a generic term for prepared raw fish. You can use tuna, salmon, lemon sole, Dover sole, sea bass, sea bream, prawns, squid, cuttlefish, bonito, or even the roe of herring and salmon. Whichever fish you choose, it must be very fresh. *Sashimi* makes a good starter at dinner parties.

---

¹/₂ lb salmon	shoyu
¹/₂ lb sea bass	2 inch piece daikon (long
2 lemon sole fillets	white radish), peeled
I tsp wasabi (green	and shredded
horse-radish powder)	

You can guarantee freshness by going to a local fishmarket. Have the fish dealer gut, fillet and skin the fish for you. You then have only to slice the fish into bite-size pieces. Flat fish such as sole should be paper thin and sea bass and bream ¹/₂ inch thick. Tuna should be cut into bite-size pieces about ¹/₂ inch thick. Squid and cuttlefish should be skinned and then cut into strips 2 inch long and ¹/₄ inch wide. Skin and bone salmon and sea bass, and cut into two from the back to the center of the bone. Slice each fillet crosswise into pieces ¹/₂ inch thick. Fillet and skin the lemon sole and slice very thinly across, with the blade held diagonally towards the fish.

Put the *wasabi* powder in an egg cup, add a little water and stir vigorously; the consistency should be firm, but not lumpy. Keep the egg cup well covered until serving time, or the pungency of the *wasabi* will be lost.

Arrange the fish decoratively on a large serving platter or wooden board and garnish with the shredded *daikon*. Mold the *wasabi* into a small mound and place on the serving platter or board. Guests should mix a little of the *wasabi* with *shoyu*, then partially dip a slice of *sashimi* into this pungent sauce before eating. If you submerge the *sashimi* in the sauce it will taste very salty. Another way of avoiding this is to dilute the *shoyu* with a little water.

Tempura

Deep-fried Fish and Vegetables

Tempura is a famous Japanese dish. Do not deep-fry the ingredients for longer than stated in the recipe as they will continue to cook after they have been removed from the oil.

---

8 headless uncooked prawns, defrosted if frozen	**Tentsuyu sauce**
1 medium squid, cleaned	1 cup dashi (see page 4)
8 button mushrooms	1/4 cup shoyu
4 oz French beans, trimmed	1/4 cup mirin (sweet rice wine) or sweet sherry
1 small eggplant, trimmed	**To serve**
vegetable oil, for deep-frying	1 inch piece fresh root ginger, peeled and grated
plain flour, for coating	3 inch piece daikon (long white radish), peeled and grated
Batter	1 lime or lemon, cut into wedges
1 egg	
3 tbsp plain flour	
1 tbsp cornstarch	

Wash and shell the prawns, retaining the tail shell. Take the black vein out, then make a slit along the belly to prevent the prawns curling during cooking. Skin the squid and cut in half. With a sharp knife, make fine diagonal slits on the outside to prevent curling during cooking. Cut the body into 2 x 1½ inch pieces.

Make the batter immediately before frying: mix the egg and ½ cup ice-cold water in a bowl, then sift in the plain flour and cornstarch. Mix very briefly, using 2 pairs of *hashi* or a fork. Do not overmix: there should still be lumps in the flour.

Put a wire rack over a roasting tin and place by the side of the stove. Heat the oil in a deep frying pan to about 325°F. Dip the mushrooms in the batter, deep-fry in the hot oil for 1 minute, then take up onto the rack to drain. Dip 3 or 4 French beans together in the batter, deep-fry for 1 minute. Halve the eggplant lengthways and slice into ½ inch thick half-moon shapes. Dip into the batter, fry for 1 minute and put on the rack above.

Increase the temperature of the oil to about 350°F. Hold the prawns by their tails and dip them into the batter one at a time (do not batter the tail shell). Deep-fry for about 1 minute, then drain on rack. Coat the squid pieces with flour, dip them in the batter and deep-fry in the hot oil for 1 minute. Remove and drain on rack.

To make the sauce bring the *dashi* to a boil in a small saucepan with the *shoyu* and *mirin*, then pour into 4 small bowls. Arrange the fried fish and vegetables on kitchen paper in a bamboo dish or serving platter with 4 piles of grated ginger and *daikon*. Garnish with lime wedges and serve immediately, with individual bowls of sauce. Each person mixes ginger and *daikon* to taste in the sauce, then dips the *tempura* into it before eating.

Tatsuta-Age

Fried Marinated Mackerel

Tatsuta-age is a method of frying. In this recipe the fish is
marinated before frying to give it extra flavor. Any type of
fish, meat or poultry, can be used.

1 large mackerel, total weight about 1 lb, filleted	1 medium piece of root ginger, peeled and grated
4 tbsp shoyu	2 oz cornstarch
2 tbsp saké	vegetable oil, for deep-frying
	4 lemon wedges to garnish

Using tweezers, remove all the bones which are hidden in the
center of the mackerel fillets. Place the fillets skin side down
on a board and cut slightly on the diagonal into slices about
1 inch thick. Put the *shoyu* in a shallow dish with the *saké* and
grated ginger and mix well. Add the mackerel slices, cover and
leave to marinate for about 10 minutes, turning occasionally
to ensure that all slices are evenly marinated. Drain the
mackerel thoroughly, then coat in some of the cornstarch.
Deep-fry the mackerel slices at about 325°F, turning once,
until golden brown. Remove from the oil and place on paper
towels.

Arrange a few slices of mackerel on each of 4 warmed
individual plates, garnished with a lemon wedge and cooked
vegetables or green salad.

Yakitori

Grilled Skewered Chicken

Yakitori is really an accompaniment for *saké*; *yakitori* bars are very popular drinking places in Japan. It is usually served in Japan as a starter but is also good for a barbecue.

---

2 chicken legs, boned
2 thin leeks, white part only, or 2 large spring onions
8 bamboo skewers
4 lemon wedges and watercress to garnish
Taré sauce
5 tbsp shoyu
2 tbsp mirin or sweet sherry
2 tbsp sugar
2 tsp plain flour

Bone the chicken legs and cut the meat into 24 bite-size pieces. Cut the leeks or spring onions into 16 pieces. Put all the ingredients for the *taré* sauce in a small saucepan. Bring to a boil, stirring, then simmer for 10 minutes, or until the sauce reduces to about two-thirds of its original volume. Remove from the heat. Thread 3 pieces of chicken and 2 pieces of leek or spring onion alternately on to 8 Japanese bamboo skewers. Grill over a charcoal barbecue or under a conventional grill until both sides brown, then remove from the heat and spoon on the *taré* sauce. Return to the heat for a few more minutes, then remove and coat with more sauce. Repeat this process a few times until all of the *taré* sauce is used and the chicken is cooked. Arrange in the center of a large plate garnished with watercress and lemon wedges.

Shoga-Yaki

Ginger Pork

This grilled ginger pork is an easy, economical dish which makes a typical Japanese lunch or family dinner accompanied by plain boiled rice and *miso* soup.

---

1 lb pork fillets or chops, boned
2 inch piece fresh root ginger, peeled and grated
4 tbsp shoyu

To grate the root ginger, ideally you need a Japanese *daikon* grater, but you can use a cheese grater, holding a dish beneath to catch the grated ginger and its juice. Slice the pork diagonally very thinly into bite-size pieces and lay them on a large plate. Sprinkle the grated ginger and juice and *shoyu* over the pork and marinate for at least 10 minutes. Heat a frying pan, add a little oil and shallow fry both sides of the pork slices. Place a few slices each on warmed individual plates, pour the juice from the pan on the pork and serve hot, garnished with boiled green vegetables and accompanied by a bowl of boiled rice.

Chicken Teriyaki

Grilled Glazed Chicken

Teriyaki means glazed grill and its effect is obtained from the sweet *taré* sauce. You can make *teriyaki* with chicken, beef or a firm fish like mackerel, cod steak, or coley. It is a delicious family meal or party dish.

---

4 chicken thighs, boned	I tbsp sugar
3 tbsp vegetable oil	watercress sprigs, to garnish
I tbsp mirin *or* sweet sherry	
Marinade	
5 tbsp shoyu	2 tbsp mirin *or* sweet sherry
2 tbsp saké *(rice wine)*	2 tsp ginger juice

Prick the chicken skin with a fork to prevent it shrinking during cooking. Put the chicken in a shallow dish. Mix together the ingredients for the marinade, pour over the chicken and leave to marinate for 20–30 minutes. Heat the oil in a frying pan. Remove the chicken from the marinade, place skin side down in the pan and fry until the skin is lightly browned. Turn the chicken over and continue frying for about 10 minutes, until the chicken is tender when pierced with *hashi*. Remove the chicken from the pan and keep warm. Add the marinade to the pan, then the additional *mirin* and sugar. Simmer for 2–3 minutes. Transfer the chicken to a board and slice thinly. Arrange the slices on a warmed serving platter, pour over the thickened marinade and garnish with watercress. Serve hot.

Wafu Roast Beef

Roast Beef Japanese-style

Japanese roast beef is traditionally served with finely chopped spring onions and grated fresh root ginger. Each person mixes a little spring onion and ginger with some of the sauce, then dips a slice of meat into it before eating. Mustard can be substituted for the ginger and spring onion.

1 1/2 lb sirloin of beef	**To serve**
1 garlic clove, peeled and sliced	2 spring onions, trimmed
1/2 cup shoyu	and finely chopped
1/2 cup saké	1 inch piece fresh root
1 1/2 tsp sugar	ginger, peeled and grated
	parsley sprigs, to garnish

Choose a long narrow beef joint and take off all the outer fat. Put it in a deep saucepan with the garlic, *shoyu*, *saké* and sugar. Place an *otoshi-buta* (small wooden lid) or small upturned plate on top of the joint, cover the pan with a lid, place over high heat and bring to a boil. Lower the heat and simmer for 10 minutes, shaking the saucepan occasionally so that the meat does not stick. Transfer the meat to a board, cut in half and check the extent of the cooking. If the meat is too rare for your liking cook for a further few minutes. Remove the saucepan from the heat and leave the meat to cool in the liquid, covered. Slice the meat thinly, then arrange on individual plates. Garnish with parsley sprigs. Serve cold in individual bowls, with the cooking liquid from the meat, and the prepared spring onions and ginger.

Tonkatsu

Fried Pork Cutlet

Breaded and deep-fried pork cutlet makes a simple, economical and extremely delicious family supper, lunch, or party dish. It is also very filling. *Tonkatsu* sauce can be bought at Japanese shops, but any ready-made fruit sauce will do.

4 boneless pork chops	4 oz dried breadcrumbs
salt	vegetable oil, for deep-frying
freshly-ground black pepper	thick fruit sauce diluted with
plain flour, for coating	shoyu, or Worcester sauce
1 egg, lightly beaten	mustard

Sprinkle the pork lightly with salt and pepper, then dust with flour, shaking off any excess. Dip each piece of pork into the beaten eggs, then coat in the breadcrumbs.

Heat the oil in a deep frying pan to 350°F. Gently slide in the pork chops one at a time. Deep-fry in batches for 5–7 minutes, turning every so often until both sides become golden brown, then remove with a perforated spoon and drain on a sheet of kitchen paper spread over a plate. When all the pieces of pork have been cooked, place them on a cutting board and cut each one cross-wise into $1/2$–1 inch wide strips. Arrange the pieces of one chop on each plate garnished with cooked vegetables or salad. Serve immediately, with the *tonkatsu* sauce in small individual dishes for dipping, and a pot of mustard.

Sukiyaki

Pan-cooked Beef with Vegetables

Most Japanese families have special *sukiyaki* pans to cook this popular hot-pot dish at the table, but a heavy-based frying pan and a portable cooking stove will do the job just as well. *Sukiyaki* is very informal – the host or hostess cooks the first amount of meat and vegetables at the table. After this first "cooking" each person serves him or herself, adding ingredients to the pan every so often.

I lb sirloin or topside of beef	½ oz shirataki (*yam-flour noodles*), or fine vermicelli
4 Chinese leaves	I small piece of beef fat
½ lb spinach	**To serve**
2 thin leeks, white part only, or 3 large spring onions	dashi (*see page 4*) or water
	shoyu
8 fresh shiitake or button mushrooms	mirin or sweet sherry
	saké
I cake firm tofu (*bean curd*)	sugar
	4 eggs (*optional*)

Freeze the meat for 1–2 hours, leave for 30 minutes on a board, then cut into wafer-thin slices 1½ inch wide and 3 inch long with a very sharp knife. Arrange the meat in a fan on a round platter. Cover and keep in the refrigerator.

Wash the Chinese leaves, cut in half lengthways, then cut into 2 inch lengths. Wash, trim and chop the spinach into 1½ inch lengths. Slice the leeks diagonally. Wipe and trim the mushrooms, cutting in half if large. Cut the *tofu* into 8 cubes. Cook the *shirataki* (if used) in boiling water for 3 minutes, then

drain. If using vermicelli, soak it in boiling water for 10 minutes, drain and then roughly cut. Arrange the vegetables, *tofu* and *shirataki* on a platter.

Place a cast-iron frying pan on a portable cooking stove in the center of the dining table. Surround with the platters of raw ingredients and with jugs of *dashi*, *shoyu*, *mirin* and *saké*, and a pot of sugar. Melt a little beef fat in the pan, then add a few slices of meat and cook until lightly browned. Add a selection of the other raw ingredients, then pour in *dashi*, *shoyu*, *mirin*, *saké* and sugar to taste. Each diner beats an egg lightly in his or her bowl, takes a selection of the cooked ingredients and dips into the beaten egg before eating.

Shabu Shabu

Beef Hot-Pot

The ingredients for *shabu shabu* are basically the same as for *sukiyaki* (see page 36), but they are cooked in a broth. The name *shabu shabu* comes from the sound of washing: wafer-thin slices of beef are picked up with *hashi*, dipped in the broth and swished from side to side as if washing clothes in water. The skill of eating *shabu shabu* lies in dexterity with *hashi*.

---

1 lb sirloin or topside of beef	4 inch square konbu
4 Chinese leaves	**Daikon sauce**
1/2 lb spinach	2 spring onions, finely chopped
8 fresh shiitake or button mushrooms	1 small daikon, peeled and grated
1 cake firm tofu	4 lemon wedges
	1/4 pt shoyu

39

Sesame sauce

3 tbsp tahini *(sesame paste)*	1 tbsp mirin *or sweet sherry*
or smooth peanut butter	2 tsp sugar
¹/₂ cup dashi *(see page 4)*	1 tbsp saké
2 tbsp shoyu	1 tsp chilli oil *(optional)*

Prepare the meat, Chinese leaves, leeks, spinach, mushrooms and *tofu* as for *sukiyaki* (see page 36). Arrange the meat, *tofu* and vegetables on a large serving platter.

Make the *daikon* sauce by grating the *daikon* and finely chopping the spring onions. Make the sesame sauce by mixing the sesame paste (or peanut butter) with the *dashi, shoyu, mirin,* sugar and *saké* in a serving bowl. Add the chilli oil for a slightly more pungent flavor, if desired.

Put the *konbu* in a earthenware pot or cast iron casserole and fill two-thirds full with cold water. Bring to a boil and immediately remove the *konbu*. Transfer the pot or casserole to a portable cooking stove in the center of the dining table and bring the water to a boil again. Put the platter of meat, *tofu* and vegetables on the table, with individual dishes of sesame sauce and bowls of chopped spring onions, grated *daikon* and lemon wedges. Pour the *shoyu* into a small jug. Set the table so that each guest has 2 sauce dishes, one for the sesame sauce and the other for the *daikon* sauce, which guests make themselves by mixing together spring onions, *daikon*, a squeeze of lemon juice and *shoyu* to taste. Guests cook the ingredients themselves in the hot broth, dipping them in the sauces before eating.

Sumeshi

Vinegared Rice

The term *sushi* is a corruption of *sumeshi*, meaning vinegared rice, which is used for all *sushi* dishes. *Nigiri-zushi*, hand-molded *sushi* with a piece of raw fish on top (see page 43), is the most famous of all.

---

2 cups Japanese short grain rice
1/4 cup rice vinegar
1 1/2 tbsp sugar
1 tsp salt
plain boiled rice (see page 4)

Cook rice (see page 4). Put the rice vinegar, sugar, and salt in a bowl and mix well until the sugar and salt have dissolved. Transfer the boiled rice to a large, preferably wooden, bowl and pour the vinegar mixture over. Using a wooden spatula or Japanese rice paddle, fold the vinegar into the rice; do not stir. Cool to room temperature before using.

Gomoku-Zushi

Sushi with Five Ingredients

Gomoku means "five kinds", though Japanese do not normally limit themselves to this number. Rice cooked in this way is usually served for a party.

1/4 lb smoked salmon	2 oz snow peas or
3 dried shiitake *mushrooms*	French beans, cooked
I small carrot, peeled	I egg
and shredded	I tbsp vegetable oil
3 tbsp sugar	2 cups sumeshi (see page 43)
3 tbsp shoyu	I sheet nori (dried lava
2 tbsp mirin or sweet sherry	paper) or cress to garnish

Shred the smoked salmon into 2 inch long strips. Soak the mushrooms in warm water for 30 minutes, then drain, reserving the liquid. Squeeze the mushrooms dry, discard the hard stalks, then finely shred. Place both mushroom and carrot shreds in a saucepan with 3 tbsp of the sugar, the *shoyu, mirin* and the *shiitake* juice. Simmer until ingredients are cooked. Lightly boil the snow peas and cut into thin strips.

Beat the egg in a small bowl, add I tsp of sugar and a pinch of salt. Heat a heavy-based frying pan and lightly oil the base. Pour in the beaten egg, tilting the pan so that it spreads evenly over the base. Fry over the lowest possible heat for 30 seconds, or until the surface of the mixture is dry. Turn the omelette on to a board and cut into thin serving strips 2 inch long.

Put the *sumeshi* in a large, preferably wooden, serving bowl. Add the mushrooms, carrot, snow peas and smoked salmon together with the cooking juice from the carrots and *shiitake*. Using a wooden spatula, gently fold the ingredients into the rice; do not stir. Sprinkle on the omelette strips. Grill the sheet of *nori* holding the edges by hand under the lowest possible heat for only a second until crisp, turning once, then shred into I–2 inch strips with kitchen scissors. Arrange the *nori* shreds on top of the rice before serving.

Nigiri-Zushi

Handmade Sushi

This hand-molded *sushi* is one of Japan's most popular snacks and originates in Tokyo. Fresh tuna, sea bass or almost any type of fish, shellfish, herring or salmon roe can be used to top small handfuls of "sticky" rice.

---

2 *cups* sumeshi (see *page 43*)
I tsp wasabi *powder*
30 small slices of assorted raw fish
shoyu
(makes 30)

Mold 2 tbsp of the *sumeshi* into a compact oval shape about 2 inch long with your hands. Repeat to make 30 ovals. Put the *wasabi* powder into an egg cup, add 2 tsp of water and stir; the consistency should be firm but not lumpy. Spread a little *wasabi* on to the top of each rice ball then cover with a slice of fish, pressing it down firmly with the fingers. Arrange the *nigiri-zushi* on 4 plates. Dilute the *shoyu* with a little water and pour onto 4 small plates. To eat, dip *sushi* in the *shoyu*.

Saba-Zushi

Mackerel Sushi

Salted and vinegared mackerel in combination with vinegared rice
makes a terrific starter. All my dinner guests, western or eastern,
adore it.

I small fresh mackerel, filleted	*I cup* sumeshi *(see page 43)*
salt	*lemon slices and cress*
rice vinegar	*to garnish*

Cover mackerel fillets completely with salt. Leave for several
hours or overnight. Remove the fillets and rub salt off roughly with
paper towels. Lay the mackerel fillets, skin side up in a dish and pour
rice vinegar over them until just covered. Leave for about 30
minutes. Take out the mackerel and wash away any remaining salt
with vinegar. Using your fingers and working from the tail end,
remove the transparent skin from each fillet, leaving the silver
pattern on the flesh intact. Carefully remove all the bones with
tweezers.

Place one of the mackerel fillets, skin side down, on the bottom
of a wooden mold, or rectangular container about 10 x 3 x 2 inches,
lined with a large gauze cloth. Fill any gaps with small pieces from
the other fillet. Press the *sumeshi* down firmly on top of the fish with
your hands. Place the wooden lid on top of the mold (or fold in the
gauze cloth) and put a weight on top. Leave in a cool place (not
the refrigerator) for a few hours or overnight. Remove from
container, unwrap, and slice into bite-size pieces. Arrange on a large
serving dish, garnished with lemon slices and cress. Serve with a small
amount of *shoyu* diluted with water on individual plates.

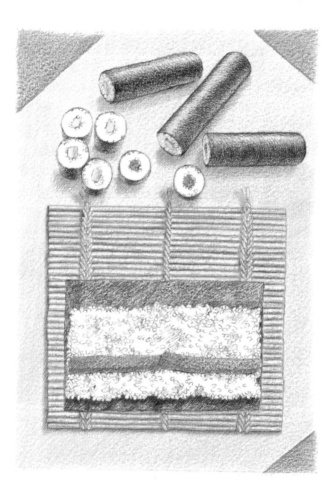

Nori-Maki

Rolled Sushi

Nori-maki are the Japanese equivalent of sandwiches and, like sandwiches, they are good for picnic lunches. There is a variety of thicknesses — *futo-maki* (thick rolls), *chubuto* (medium rolls) and *hoso-maki* (thin rolls) — depending on how you roll the *nori* sheets and which size sheet you use. The standard whole sheet is 10 x 5 inch but you can use half. Almost any ingredient can be used: smoked salmon, ham, cheese, fried bacon or sausage or even canned food such as sardines, tuna, salmon or anchovies. This recipe shows how to make *hoso-maki* using the three most popular ingredients.

$^{1}/_{2}$ cucumber
$^{1}/_{4}$ lb fresh raw tuna or salmon
I small pkt takuan (*pickled diakon*)
3 sheets nori (*dried lava paper*)
sumeshi (*see page 43*)
I tsp wasabi powder (*optional*)

Cut the cucumber, tuna and *takuan* into long sticks about $^{1}/_{4}$ inch thick. Grill *nori* sheets lightly on both sides by holding for a few seconds over the lowest possible heat and moving continuously so as to grill evenly. This brings out the flavor and makes the *nori* crisp. Cut in half. Put a half sheet of *nori*, longest side nearest to you, on a *makisu* (special roll-up bamboo mat) or a large thick piece of paper. Place a handful of *sumeshi* in the center of the *nori* and spread it with your fingers, leaving a $^{1}/_{4}$ inch margin on the side nearest to you and $^{1}/_{2}$ inch on the side opposite.

Place a stick of cucumber across the rice about one-third from the side nearest to you. Roll up the *makisu* or paper from your side so that the cucumber is in the center of the *nori-maki*, taking care not to roll in the mat or the paper. Repeat this for other ingredients making 2 rolls for each, and cut each roll into 6 pieces. If you like a hot taste, mix the *wasabi* powder with a little water and put a very small amount on each strip of cucumber and tuna (or salmon).

Oyako Donburi

Rice with Chicken and Egg

Oyako means parent-child and this dish is so named because the recipe uses chicken and egg. *Donburi* often refers to a large bowl of rice topped with poultry, meat or fish.

Gohan (see page 4) made with	5 tbsp shoyu
3 cups Japanese short grain rice	2 tbsp saké
2 medium onions	1 tbsp mirin or sweet sherry
4 spring onions	1 tbsp sugar
1/2 lb boneless chicken	4 eggs
breast meat, skinned	watercress, roughly chopped,
2 cups dashi (see page 4)	to garnish

Cut the onions in half and slice thinly. Cut the spring onions in half lengthways, and then cut the remainder into 2 inch strips. Chop the chicken into bite-size pieces. Mix the *dashi* with the *shoyu*, *saké*, *mirin* and sugar and stir well. Divide the *gohan* equally between 4 individual bowls or plates. Pour a

quarter of the *dashi* mixture into a small, heavy-based frying pan. Add a quarter of the thinly sliced onions and bring to a boil, then add a quarter of the chicken meat and cook for 2 minutes. Add a quarter of the spring onions, cook for a few seconds, then pour in one beaten egg. Cook until only just set, then put on top of one bowl of *gohan*. Repeat with remaining ingredients to make 4 *oyako donburi*. Garnish with chopped watercress.

Mori Soba

Noodles with Sauce

Soba is a thin greyish-brown noodle made from buckwheat. It is an ideal dish for a quick lunch in a busy day.

12 oz dried soba	2 spring onions, finely
1 cup dashi (see page 4)	chopped
1/2 cup shoyu	1 tsp wasabi powder
1 tbsp mirin or sweet sherry	1 sheet nori to garnish
1 tsp sugar	

Boil about 4 pts of water in a large saucepan and add the *soba*. Bring to a boil, lower the heat to prevent overflowing and gently boil for 6 minutes. Drain in a colander, wash away the starch in cold water and drain well. Heat the *dashi* in a saucepan, add the *shoyu, mirin* and sugar, and pour into 4 small cups. Put the *wasabi* in an egg cup, add a little water and stir well to make a paste. Put the *soba* on 4 individual bamboo dishes or plates, and sprinkle over the lightly grilled and shredded *nori*.

Place the chopped spring onions and *wasabi* paste on separate dishes. Serve the sauce hot or cold in individual bowls. Each person mixes some spring onion and *wasabi* into the sauce and dips it small amounts of *soba* into the sauce before eating.

Kakitama Udon

Thick Noodle Soup with Eggs

This is an excellent quick lunch dish. As the thickened soup is very warming, it is particularly suitable in cold weather.

12 oz udon (thick dried noodles)	2 tbsp cornstarch
4 cups dashi (see page 4)	4 eggs, beaten
4 tbsp shoyu	2 spring onions, finely chopped
2 tbsp mirin or sweet sherry	shichimi (7 spice condiment, optional)
1 tsp salt	

Boil the *udon* as for *soba* (see page 55) but for 10–15 minutes until soft (but not soggy). Drain and wash away the starch in cold water. Heat the *dashi* in a saucepan with the *shoyu*, *mirin* and salt. Mix the cornstarch with a $1/2$ cup of water, and add to the pan a little at a time, stirring all the while until the soup thickens slightly. Slowly add the eggs to the soup, then cook over a low heat until strands of egg float to the surface. Remove the saucepan from the heat. Pour hot water onto the drained *udon* to reheat and then divide equally between 4 individual noodle bowls. Pour the egg soup over the noodles and garnish with the chopped spring onions. Serve hot, with *shichimi* pepper.

Drinks and Desserts

Many Japanese start a meal with lager beer to accompany hors d'oeuvre, and sometimes switch to *saké* with the main dishes. Bowls of boiled rice, soup and pickled vegetables are served at the end of a dinner-party meal, but not until the host is satisfied all the guests have had enough *saké*. In a sense, the serving of rice is a signal to stop drinking. By then the guest is quite full and can only just manage the rice and soup. The Japanese did not develop any European-type desserts. Instead, a selection of fresh fruits is normally served to refresh the mouth and clear the mind. Green tea completes the meal.

Saké *Saké*, a distilled rice wine, occupies a central place in Japanese life. Wine complements food, but in Japan food complements *saké*. It can be drunk either cold or warm. *Saké* is normally drunk from a tiny cup called an *ochoko* or *guinomi*, but you can use an egg cup.

Ocha Most Japanese tea retains the green color of the original tea leaves because it is steamed. We so cherish our green tea (*cha*) that we respectfully address it with the prefix "o", *ocha*. There are many kinds of *ochas*, not just classified by grade but also by region and age. The most delicate (and expensive) tea is *gyokuro* (morning dew drop), which is shaped like a tiny peppercorn. The most popular is called *sencha* and the most common, supermarket, tea, a grilled, slightly-brown tea, is called *bancha*. The finer the tea, the lower the temperature of the water. Apart from daily teas there are special teas such as *matcha*, a powdered tea used in the tea ceremony, and *mugicha*, a barley tea used as a cold drink in summer.

Index